The American Flag

Jennifer Silate

The Rosen Publishing Group's
PowerKids Press™
PRIMARY SOURCE

Published in 2006 by The Rosen Publishing Group, Inc.
29 East 21st Street, New York, NY 10010

Editor: Eric Fein
Book Design: Michael DeLisio
Photo Researcher: Amy Feinberg

Photo Credits: cover © New York Historical Society, New York, USA/Bridgeman Art Library; p. 4 Library of Congress Geography and Map Division, (inset); p.11 Library of Congress Prints and Photographs Division; p. 7 Print Collection, Miriam and Ira D. Wallach Division of Art, Prints and Photographs, The New York Public Library, Astor, Lenox and Tilden Foundations, (inset) © North Wind Picture Archives; p. 8 Archives Charmet/Bridgeman Art Library, (inset) Courtesy of Tryon Palace Historic Sites & Gardens, New Bern, NC; p. 11 (inset) © Atwater Kent Museum of Philadelphia/Bridgeman Art Library; p. 12 Kentucky Historical Society, (inset) Old Military and Civil Records, National Archives; p. 15 Armed Forces History Collection, National Museum of American History, Behring Center, Smithsonian Institution, (inset) Smithsonian Institution, National Museum of American History, © 2002; p. 16 (left) Library of Congress Music Division, (right) The Walters Art Museum, Baltimore; p. 19 National Archives, (inset); p. 20 © AP/Wide World Photos.

First Edition

Library of Congress Cataloging-in-Publication Data

Silate, Jennifer.
    The American flag / Jennifer Silate.— 1st ed.
    p. cm. — (Primary sources of American symbols)
    Includes bibliographical references (p.) and index.
    Contents: Early flags in America — The flags of war — The Grand Union
    flag — Making the American flag — Making it official — The flag and
    the War of 1812 — Francis Scott Key and the Star-spangled banner —
    Congress changes the flag — Honoring the flag — Timeline.
    ISBN 1-4042-2686-9 (lib. bdg.)
    1. Flags—United States—History—Juvenile literature. [1.
    Flags—United States—History.] I. Title. II. Series: Silate,
    Jennifer. Primary sources of American symbols.

    CR113.S5 2006
    929.9'2'0973—dc22
                                        2003019250

Manufactured in the United States of America

Contents

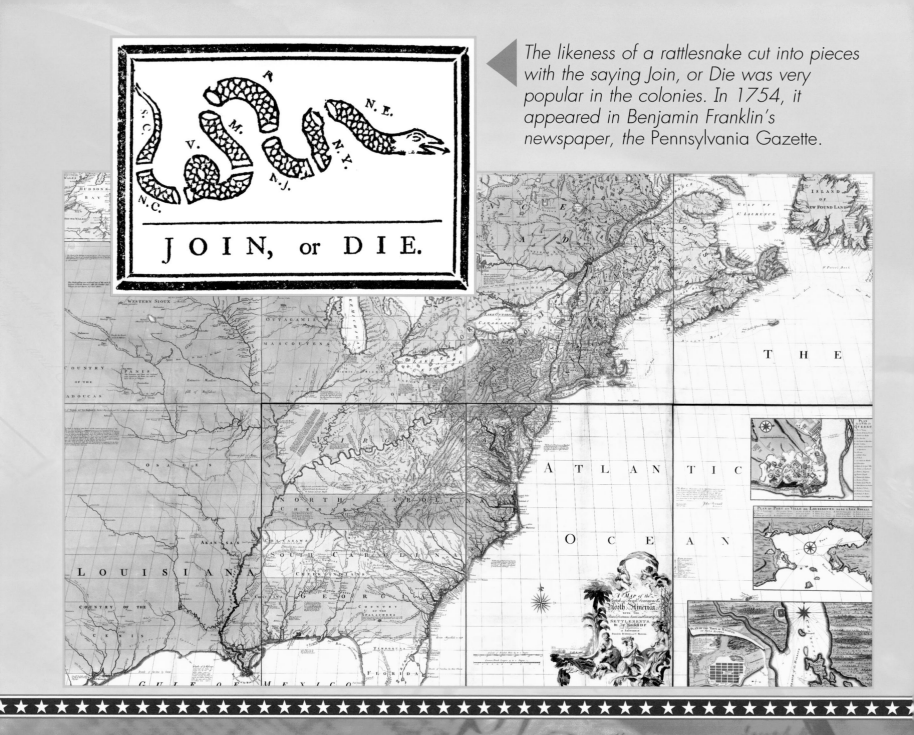

The likeness of a rattlesnake cut into pieces with the saying *Join, or Die* was very popular in the colonies. In 1754, it appeared in Benjamin Franklin's newspaper, *the Pennsylvania Gazette.*

Early Flags in America

The American flag has its roots in colonial times. Between 1607 and 1733, England set up 13 colonies on the east coast of North America. British flags, including the Union Jack, were flown in the colonies to show that England ruled them.

England placed high taxes on the colonies. This angered the colonists. The colonists made a flag to help unify them against England. The flag showed a rattlesnake cut into pieces. Each piece stood for a colony. Below the snake, Join, or Die was written. Just as the snake could not live when cut into pieces, the flag warned that the colonies could not **survive** alone. They would have to be united in their stand against England.

This map shows England's colonies on the east coast of North America. The map was printed in the late 1750s or early 1760s.

The Flags of War

  War broke out between the colonies and England on April 19, 1775. This war was called the **American Revolutionary War**. During the war, the colonists used many different flags. Some American warships flew a flag that showed a rattlesnake and the words Don't Tread On Me. The flag had a field of red and white stripes.

  The governing body of the colonies was called the **Continental Congress**. In late 1775, the congress formed a group to **design** an official flag. The flag they designed was called the Continental flag. It was also known as the Grand Union flag.

The Battle of Lexington was the first battle of the American Revolutionary War. This picture of the battle was made by Amos Doolittle. He based his picture on the reports of the fighting from people who were there.

There were many different designs for the *Don't Tread On Me* flag. Sometimes, the rattlesnake would be shown curled up. Other flags, like this one, showed the snake stretched out.

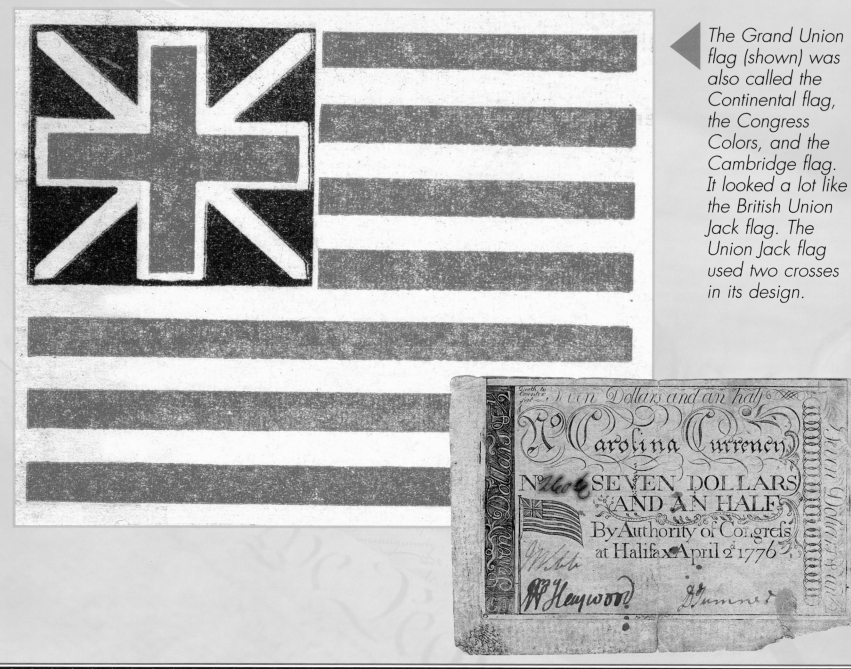

The Grand Union flag (shown) was also called the Continental flag, the Congress Colors, and the Cambridge flag. It looked a lot like the British Union Jack flag. The Union Jack flag used two crosses in its design.

The Grand Union Flag

The Continental flag used the Union Jack in its design. This might be why some people called it the Grand Union flag. This flag was used by the colonies' army, the **Continental army**. General George Washington was in charge of this army. In 1776, he flew the Grand Union flag over his base in Massachusetts. At the time, the British and American armies were fighting each other. However, the British army thought the flag Washington was flying was a British flag. They thought this meant that Washington wanted to give up the battle. The flag was not used for very long because of the **confusion** it caused. A new American flag was soon made. This flag was different from the British flag.

The Grand Union flag became an important symbol to the colonists. They even used it on their paper money, such as this seven-and-a-half dollar bill from North Carolina.

Making the American Flag

No one knows exactly who made the first American flag. A man named Francis Hopkinson is often given credit for designing the flag. Hopkinson was a lawyer. His design for the flag had 13 stars and 13 red and white stripes. This is why the flag is called the Stars and Stripes.

Many people believe Betsy Ross played an important role in making the first flag. Ross was an **upholsterer**. It is believed that George Washington and two other men came to her store in Philadelphia, Pennsylvania, in June 1776. While there, they asked her to make the flag. However, there are no records of her having sewn the flag. We may never know who truly made the first American flag.

There is little proof to support the claim that Betsy Ross (second from left) made the first Stars and Stripes flag. However, this story has become a part of American history. General George Washington (center) is shown here, looking over the finished flag.

Francis Hopkinson was a lawyer, a writer, and a musician. He represented New Jersey in the Continental Congress in 1776 and signed the Declaration of Independence.

Secretary of Congress Charles Thomson took notes at the meeting where the flag resolution was passed. His notes were kept in a Continental Congress journal.

Resolved That the Flag of the united states consist of 13 stripes alternate red and white, that the Union be 13 stars white in a blue field representing a new constellation. —

The Council of the state of Massachusetts bay having represented by letter to the president

Making It Official

The Continental Congress made the Stars and Stripes the official flag of the United States on June 14, 1777. Congress passed a **resolution**, or notice, stating that the new flag would have 13 stars and 13 red and white stripes. The 13 stars and stripes on the flag stood for the 13 colonies that made up the new country. Congress did not state how the stars or stripes should be placed on the flag. This led to the design of many different flags that used stars and stripes.

When the American Revolutionary War ended in 1783, America became free of England's rule. By 1795, Vermont and Kentucky joined the United States. Two more stars and two more stripes were added to the flag.

Vermont became a state in 1791. Kentucky joined the United States in 1792. Two more stars and two more stripes were added to the flag, bringing the totals to 15.

The Flag and the War of 1812

The flag now had 15 stars and 15 stripes. This version of the flag was to be used for the next 23 years, until 1818. In 1812, America again found itself at war with England. This war was called the **War of 1812**. One of the war's causes was that the U.S. government was angered because England was causing trouble to American ships at sea. America won the war, which ended on February 17, 1815.

One of the most important battles of the war happened on the night of September 13, 1814, in Baltimore, Maryland. British ships attacked Fort McHenry, pounding it with cannonball fire. However, the star-shaped fort stood up to the furious attack. Even the gigantic American flag that flew over the fort survived the attack. This flag was 30 feet (9.1 m) by 42 feet (12.8 m).

Fort McHenry was named after James McHenry. McHenry was one of the people who signed the U.S. Constitution. He was also Secretary of War from 1796 to 1800.

The flag that survived the British attack on Fort McHenry was made by Mary Pickersgill.

The Star-spangled banner.

O! say, can ye see by the dawn's early light
What so proudly we hail'd by the twilight's last gleaming?
Whose bright stars & broad stripes, through the clouds of the fight,
O'er the ramparts we watch'd were so gallantly streaming?
And the rocket's red glare, the bombs bursting in air,
Gave proof through the night that our flag was still there.
O! say does that star-spangled banner yet wave
O'er the land of the free & the home of the brave?

On that shore, dimly seen through the mists of the deep,
Where the foe's haughty host in dread silence reposes,
What is that which the breeze, o'er the towering steep,
As it fitfully blows, half-conceals, half-discloses?
Now it catches the gleam of the morning's first beam,
In full glory reflected, now shines on the stream.
'Tis the star-spangled banner O! long may it wave
O'er the land of the free & the home of the brave.

And where is that host that so vauntingly swore
That the havoc of war & the battle's confusion
A home & a country should leave us no more?
Their blood has wash'd out their foul footstep's pollution.
No refuge could save the hireling & slave
From the terror of flight or the gloom of the grave.
And the star-spangled banner in triumph doth wave
O'er the land of the free & the home of the brave.

O! thus be it ever when freemen shall stand
Between their lov'd homes & the war's desolation.
Blest with vict'ry & peace, may the heav'n rescued land
Praise the power that hath made & preserv'd us a nation.
Then conquer we must when our cause it is just,
And this be our motto - In God is our trust.
And the star-spangled banner in triumph shall wave
O'er the land of the free and the home of the brave.

Washington
Oct 21 ____ 40.   F S Key

"The Star-Spangled Banner" was first printed with the title "Defence of Fort McHenry." It was published on September 20, 1814 in the Baltimore Patriot. The poem was soon set to music and became very popular. Key wrote out the poem for different people over the years. Pictured is a copy of "The Star-Spangled Banner" he wrote out in 1840.

Francis Scott Key and "The Star-Spangled Banner"

An American lawyer, Francis Scott Key, was being held on one of the British ships near Fort McHenry. Key had gone to Chesapeake Bay, near Baltimore, to see the British. He was trying to get them to free a friend of his whom they were holding prisoner. Instead, Key was held overnight against his will. From the ship, Key saw the British attack Fort McHenry. He saw the bombs exploding in the sky over the fort. When daylight came, Key noticed that the large American flag was still flying over the fort. He then knew the Americans had won the battle! Inspired by the sight of the flag, he wrote a poem about the battle. The poem became very popular. It was soon turned into America's **national anthem**, "The Star-Spangled Banner."

In 1833, Francis Scott Key (seen here in detail from a larger painting), worked as a lawyer for the city of Washington, D.C.

Congress Changes the Flag

By 1918, five more states had been added to the United States of America. Congress once again changed the flag. This time, though, no more stripes were added. Congress decided that the flag would have too many stripes if one were put on it for each state. They did not want to have to change the shape of the flag to add more stripes. Instead, the flag was returned to having only 13 stripes. The stripes stood for the first 13 colonies. Five new stars were added for the five new states. From then on, a star would be added to the flag for every new state.

Today, the American flag has 50 stars that stand for the 50 states in the United States of America.

This 1918 photo shows women from Russia, Germany, and other countries sewing a flag in America.

To observe the end of World War I, a parade was held in New York City, New York, on November 11, 1918. The American flag was displayed along the parade's path.

Following the September 11, 2001 terrorist attacks, firefighters raised the American flag at the remains of the World Trade Center in New York City. A picture of this scene was made into a stamp by the United States Postal Service. The "Heroes of 2001" stamp was sold to raise money for the families of the rescue workers killed or hurt during the attacks.

Honoring the Flag

People have honored the American flag in many ways. A special holiday, Flag Day, was created to **celebrate** the flag. The first Flag Day was celebrated on June 14, 1885 by a school in Wisconsin. In 1949, President Harry S. Truman made June 14 of each year National Flag Day. Today, Americans hold parades and other celebrations in honor of Flag Day.

The American flag is also used to honor people. When the president, a government leader, or other famous person dies, the flag is flown at **half-staff** on its flagpole. This is to show that the country has lost one of its heroes. The flag is an important **symbol** of America. It has even been placed on the moon!

The first American flag was planted on the moon on July 20, 1969, by Apollo 11 astronaut Neil Armstrong. Here, Apollo 15 astronaut James Irwin salutes the flag during a moonwalk in August 1971.

Timeline

1700s	The Join, or Die flag is first used.
1775–1783	Colonists fight against England in the American Revolutionary War.
1776	The Grand Union Flag is flown over George Washington's base.
June 14, 1777	Congress passes the Flag Resolution.
1795	The American flag now has 15 stars and 15 stripes.
1812–1815	America fights against England in the War of 1812.
1814	Francis Scott Key writes "The Star-Spangled Banner."
1885	The first Flag Day is held.
1918	Official American flag is returned to having only 13 stripes.
1931	"The Star-Spangled Banner" is made the national anthem.
1949	President Harry S. Truman signs congressional act for National Flag Day.

Glossary

American Revolutionary War (uh-MER-uh-kuhn rev-uh-LOO-shuh-ner-ee WOR) The war from 1775–1783 during which the American colonies fought against England. As a result, the United States of America was created.

celebrate (SEL-uh-brate) To do something enjoyable on a special occasion.

confusion (kuhn-FYOOZ-shuhn) To not understand something or know what to do about it.

Continental army (KON-tuh-nuhnt-el AR-mee) The colonial army that fought against the British in the American Revolutionary War.

Continental Congress (KON-tuh-nuhnt-el KON-gress) A group of people picked to decide laws for the American colonies.

design (di-ZINE) To draw something that could be built or made.

half-staff (HAF-STAF) To fly a flag halfway up its pole, usually to show respect for someone who has died.

national anthem (NASH-uh-nuhl AN-thuhm) The official song of a country.

resolution (rez-uh-LOO-shuhn) The formal statement of an official decision to take an action that is made by a government body.

survive (sur-VIVE) To continue to live or exist.

symbol (SIM-buhl) A design or an object that represents something else.

upholsterer (uhp-HOHL-stur-ur) A person who puts upholstery, such as cloth, on a piece of furniture.

War of 1812 (WOR OHV ATE-een-TWELV) A war from 1812–1815 between England and the United States.

Index

Primary Sources

Cover: Handmade American flag with thirteen stars [c. 1830–1880]. New York Historical Society. **Page 4 (inset):** Join, or Die. Woodcut [May 9, 1754]. Library Congress. **Page 4:** A map of the British and French dominions in North America. Mitchell [c. 1761]. Map Division of the Library of Congress. **Page 7:** Rattlesnake with Don't Tread On Me. Handcolored woodcut [Date unknown]. **Page 7:** The Ba of Lexington, April 19, 1775 [c.1775]. Colored engraving by Amos Doolittle. New York Public Library Print Collection. **Page 8:** The Grand Union Flag [Pre-twen century]. Color woodblock print. Artist unknown. Archives Charmet. **Page 8 (inset)** North Carolina $7-½ note [1776]. Tryon Palace Historic Sites & Gardens. **Page** The Birth of Old Glory [c. 1917]. A photo-mechanical print from a painting by Pe Moran. Library of Congress Prints and Photographs Division. **Page 11 (inset):** Fran Hopkinson [c. 1700s]. Oil on canvas by Robert Edge Pine. Atwater Kent Museun Philadelphia. Courtesy of the Historical Society of Pennsylvania Collection. **Page** 1795 Fifteen Star Flag [Reproduction made c. 1892]. Kentucky Historical Society **Page 12 (inset):** Continental Congress journal entry about the American flag [June 1777]. National Archives and Records Administration. **Page 15:** The Bombardme Ft. McHenry [1816]. A Lithograph by J. Bower. Armed Forces History Collection, National Museum of American History, Behring Center, Smithsonian Institution. **Pa** 15 (inset): The Star-Spangled Banner flag [c. early 1800s]. The National Museun American History, The Smithsonian Institution. **Page 16:** Francis Scott Key [c. 181 Oil painting by Joseph Wood. Walters Art Museum. **Page 16:** "The Star-Spangler Banner" [1840]. A handwritten copy by Francis Scott Key. Library of Congress. **Page 19:** Patriotic old women make flags [c. 1918]. Photographic print. Nationa Archives and Records Administration. **Page 19 (inset):** New York City street as pe celebrate Armistice Day [November 11, 1918]. Black and white photograph. Associated Press. **Page 20:** Astronaut James Irwin salutes a U.S. flag planted on th moon [August 1971]. Associated Press. **Page 20 (inset):** United States Postal Serv Stamp. The Heroes of 2001 [September 9, 2002]. Photograph of the stamp by J Brush. Associated Press.

Web Sites

Due to the changing nature of Internet links, PowerKids Press has developed an on-line list of Web sites related to the subject of this book. This site is updated regularly. Please use this link to access the list:

http://www.powerkidslinks.com/psas/taf/